Kansas Book Festival 2019 Yearbook

Kansas Book Festival
2019
Yearbook

Kansas Book Festival Yearbook
Copyright © 2019 Kansas Masonic Lodge

All rights reserved. No part of this publication may be reproduced, distributed, or transmitted in any form or by any means, without prior written permission of the copyright holder.

Published by Kellogg Press
1114 Commercial St.
Emporia, Kansas 66801
kelloggpress.com

With a grant from Ellen Plumb's City Bookstore
1122 Commercial St.
Emporia, KS 66801
ellenplumbs.com

Mary Brownback
Chair, Kansas Book Festival

Sarah Shipman
Director, Kansas Book Festival

Dr. Dennis J. Kear
Executive Director, Kansas Masonic Literacy Center

Tasia Markowitz
Assistant Director, Kansas Masonic Literacy Center

Amanda Parkman, Administrative Assistant, Kansas Masonic Literacy Center

Printed in the United States of America

Curtis Becker, Editor/Layout and Design/Cover Design
curtis@curtisbeckerbooks.com
curtisbeckerbooks.com

Lindsey Bartlett, Cover Art

ISBN: 978-0-9971142-3-2

Maddie Duncan
Newton
Grade 9   **1**
Newton High School

Chandler Fienhage
Valley Falls
Grade 11   **5**
Valley Falls High School

Elsie Fleming
Iola
Grade 8   **11**
Iola Middle School

Josie Gage
Maple City
Grade 10   **15**
Dexter High School

Dan Hardy
South Hutchinson
Grade 11   **19**
Nickerson High School

Bailey Jackson
Preston
Grade 7   **25**
Liberty Middle School

Grace Elizabeth Johnson
Maple Hill
Grade 5
Mission Valley Elementary
  29

Chase Kellogg
Galenda
Grade 12
Riverton High School
  31

Lily Kuhn
Spring Hill
Grade 10
Spring Hill High School
  37

Cashlyn Kvasnicka
Quinter
Grade 8
Quinter Junior Senior High School
  41

Callie Locke
South Haven
Grade 7
South Haven Junior High School
  43

Amelia Marten
Cheney
Grade 5
Garden Plain Elementary
  45

Yu'Nique Reed
Hutchinson
Grade 5   **47**
Magnet School at Allen

Bailey Scott
Overland Park
Grade 5   **51**
Scott Academy

Fiona Stevenson
Topeka
Grade 5   **55**
Tecumseh South Elementary School

Jessie Taylor
Iola
Grade 8   **59**
Iola Middle School

Elsie Unruh
Hutchinson
Grade 8   **63**
Huchinson Middle School

Jacob Unruh
Hutchinson
Grade 10   **67**
Hutchinson High School

Kai Waddell
Wichita
Grade 4   73
Clark Davidson Elementary School

Samson Weber
Burlingame
Grade 5   75
Silver Lake Grade School

Brendan C. Wheatley
Olathe
Grade 7   79
Frontier Trail Middle School

Ben Wieland
Shawnee
Grade 10   83
Mill Valley High School

Maggie Wieland
Shawnee
Grade 6   89
Monticello Trails Middle School

Zachary Wieland
Shawnee
Grade 3   91
Prairie Ridge Elementary School

Kansas: A Beacon for Freedom
Maddie Duncan
Grade 9
Newton High School

In the year 1855, there were 155 free African-Americans in the Kansas Territory, and in 1870 there were 17,108. By the year 1880, the African-American population in Kansas grew by 25,999, to a grand total of 43,107 people. This large increase in population was caused by a group of people trying to escape the persecution and violence in the South. They called themselves the Exodusters.

The Exodusters were free, Southern African-Americans during the time following the Civil War. After the war ended in 1865, there was still unrest in the South. African-Americans were barred from entering voting booths by white Democrats. Additionally, many wished for economic freedom, but were restricted. This is because many were only able to farm, according to historian Todd Arrington. Due to a lack of a varied skill set, many freed slaves were consequently limited in their career fields. Since they had no money to buy land, they were forced to return to work under former slave owners. According to the National Parks Service, their compensation was poor for the work they did. Along with this, there was violence against African-Americans in Southern states. Lynching was a popular way among whites to instill fear into black communities. People were often lynched for minor infractions, and without trial in many cases.

The Exodusters wanted to live in a place that was truly free, away from the discrimination that plagued them in the South. The actions of John Brown and other Kansas abolitionists also made Kansas a hopeful place for former slaves and their families. The notorious "Bleeding Kansas" conflict gave the impression that Kansan's would not tolerate such discrimination that was happening in the South. It made it seem as though Kansas was a welcoming place for all people. People saw it as a place to "freely exercise their rights as American citizens, gain true political freedom, and have the opportunity to achieve economic self-sufficiency.", according to an article about the movement by archivist Damani Davis. All of these things made Kansas seem like the perfect place to go to escape the South.

Lead by influencers like Benjamin Singleton and Henry Adams, African-Americans from many Southern States began to migrate towards Kansas. Some families made it all the way through to Kansas before settling. Others stopped their journey in Missouri or Oklahoma.

Throughout its course however, the movement garnered protests from both African-Americans and white Southerners. Despite this, it continued on for over a decade. In addition, as time went on, those who took the journey decided to name it. They called it the Exodus. It was called this in reference to the biblical Exodus, in which Moses led the Israelites out of Egypt. While it began in the 1860s and continued up until the 1880s, its year of prominence was in 1879. This year of the movement is called the Exodus of 1879, and is generally used as the representative year of the Exodus. This is due to there being the largest amount of people wishing to move into the state during this time. Between 1879 and 1880, around 20,000 people left the South enroute for Kansas. Those who completed the journey settled in towns such as Atchison, Nicodemus, and Wyandotte. Laws and acts that passed during this time contributed to the start of the Exodus. In 1859, the Wyandotte Constitution was passed in Kansas. While it did not allow African-Americans the right to vote, it prohibited slavery and allowed free African-Americans to live in the state.

Additionally, President Abraham Lincoln passed the Homestead Act of 1862, which stated that American citizens could receive a homestead from the federal government. Citizens of all races, over the age of 21, could apply to receive these 160-acre homesteads. This allowed there to be a migration into states, such as Kansas, since land was more accessible and was free of charge.

Life in Kansas turned out to be far from perfect. There was still discrimination, while not as severe as in the South, from white people in the area. Many families did not have the tools and money to start farming right away. In Nicodemus, some men had to travel as far as 55 miles for work at the Kansas Pacific Railroad. Yet, throughout all of these hardships, people stayed and survived long enough to have success in farming. Throughout the years, people were able to build cities around the settlements.

Through the actions of the Exodusters, we can see that Kansas was a place people looked to for freedom and hope. However, many people do not see Kansas as such today. Kansas is not exempt from many of the issues that plague our country today. Many of the political issues in question may, according to some, be violating and infringing upon rights we have as American citizens. Some of these issues, such as the #MeToo movement, make sexual assault victims feel as though their voices are not being heard by those in power. Others issues, such as police brutality and gun control, make people feel unsafe at school or just driving through their own towns. People should be able to live in a place where they feel safe in their homes and places of work.

Nevertheless, these issues are still debated about in our state and our country. People don't feel welcome, despite our state once being a symbol of freedom for those who are oppressed. Kansans must work together to restore our image as a state, of a place of freedom, hope, and acceptance. Everyone should feel at home in Kansas, where we head to the stars, even through the most difficult times.

Bibliography

Arrington, Todd. "Exodusters." *National Park Service*, National Park Service, 10 Apr. 2015, www.nps.gov/home/learn/historyculture/exodusters.htm.

Davis, Damani. "Exodus to Kansas." *National Archives*, National Archives, 2008, www.archives.gov/publications/prologue/2008/summer/exodus.html.

Getchell, Michelle. "The Homestead Act and the Exodusters." Khan Academy, *Khan Academy*, www.khanacademy.org/humanities/us-history/the-gilded-age/american-west/a/the-homes tead-act-and-the-exodusters.

Kansas Historical Society. "Exodusters." *KSHS*, Kansas Historical Society, June 2011, www.kshs.org/kansapedia/exodusters/17162.

Kansas Historical Society. "Wyandotte Constitution." *KSHS*, Kansas Historical Society, Apr. 2010,www.kshs.org/kansapedia/wyandotte-constitution/13884.

Roe, Jason. "Exodusters Mark the Spot." *Kansas City History*, Kansas City Public Library, www.kchistory.org/week-kansas-city-history/exodusters-mark-spot.

Weiser, Kathy. "Nicodemus -- A Black Pioneer Town." *Legends of America*, Legends of America, Nov. 2018, www.legendsofamerica.com/ks-nicodemus/2/.

To the Stars, Through Much Difficulty
Chandler Fienge
Grade 11
Valley Falls High School

On a perfect, sunny day, a Kansas resident can enjoy a perfect view of the historic Kansas State Capitol Building in Topeka. That resident can stop on the lawn just north of the building and admire the beautiful French architecture complemented by a mighty bronze statue resting atop the dome. This extraordinary figure represents the important role Native Americans played in Kansas history as this Native American warrior readies to release an arrow aiming for the sky. The warrior was coined "Ad Astra", extracted from the state motto, "Ad Astra Per Aspera". This phrase translates to: "To the stars through difficulty" . . . With the rich and exciting history belonging to Kansas, one can only interpret this motto to represent the aim taken at the goals Kansans held as they traveled through hardships like the "Bleeding Kansas" period and the American Civil War. Among these hardships, one severe and boiling-hot topic stewed in Kansans' backyards: segregation. Segregation swept through our nation, but an event in Kansas demonstrates that Kansans take aim at solving problems, even as big a problem as segregation. This event? The Brown v. Board of Education of Topeka court case.

In the late 1800s and even through the 1900s, segregation and the idea of racism quite literally divided the United States of America. The National Association for the Advancement of Colored People (NAACP) filed several court cases in Delaware, South Carolina, Virginia, and other coastal states; however, in 1951, Oliver Brown, an African-American man from Topeka filed his own lawsuit against the Topeka Board of Education.

This Kansan aimed at his goal of ending a long-standing practice that only weakens the strength of the community, state, and nation.

This event began when an all-white school in Topeka denied Brown's daughter, Linda, access, forcing her to walk several blocks to a bus stop through a violent neighborhood to attend a school further away from her home. While the school failed to give any reasonable explanation, the Supreme Court stated that denying Linda her proper education violated the 14th Amendment. Eventually, Oliver Brown's case combined with three other cases for viewing by the Supreme Court. The combined cases were known under one name: Brown v. Board of Education of Topeka and many conservative Americans of that time tried to silence this case and others like it by using the "Separate but Equal" phrase. After years of waiting, trials and mistrials, re-arguments, and several studies, the Supreme Court ruled in favor of Brown and the other plaintiffs. In reaction to his successful pleas, Brown exclaimed, "We conclude that in the field of public education the doctrine of 'separate but equal' has no place." Still, Brown and others like him would need to maintain their aim to achieve segregation.

While this verdict provided a huge triumph for Kansas and the United States as a whole, the road ahead was long and slow-moving. Kansas elementary and middle schools integrated within a year of the verdict, high schools within a year and a half, and teachers and principals integrated within two and a half years. This case makes me proud of my Kansas citizenship and gives me immeasurable faith that the United States aims to fulfill its goal of existing as a land of opportunity and equality. The everlasting effects of this case still shine through today and provide proof that Kansans truly do aim for the stars.

Most Kansans become aware of the Brown v. Board of Education case and the National Historic Site that calls Topeka home at relatively young ages. When I asked myself, *What can Kansans learn from Brown v. Board?* I immediately conclude the most appropriate answer as, *It depends on the individual.* Kansans can learn so many things about the case; but the best way to learn requires a visit the Brown v. Board National Historic Site. I've been to the National Historic Site three times in my life, and each time I am blown away. With these experiences, one can book a tour and become engulfed in a gallery of videos from the court case, reactions to the famous verdict in Washington D.C. and all over the nation, and several other incredible features. One thing that always blows my mind is the water fountains - such a small detail, but it leaves such a mark on a person to know that skin color once separated which water fountain one could drink from. To describe this museum in one word: astonishing. I would recommend this as the first place to visit upon arrival in Kansas.

Having this history right in our presence provides a great way to learn; but what is there to learn? Everything. Kansans can learn the value of being a free citizen. We can learn how to be humble, respectful, open to new ideas, and realize that every human has something to offer to this planet. Most importantly, in my opinion, Brown v. Board can help Kansans learn that religion, gender, and especially race play no role in the "value" of a human being.

With that said, Kansans learned much from this historical event. The history of Brown vs. Board exists right here with us. In other words, "the hay is in the barn". The case is settled, and the work put into the case showed the perseverance of many hard-working citizens. The next thing we must ask ourselves is: "How can this event help Kansas move forward?" In my opinion, we can start in the education system. In every history class I've taken, whether Kansas or American, the Brown vs. Board case is hardly touched on, if at all. Segregation stands as a topic that doesn't allow for much discussion, in my experiences, because it is considered "touchy". I feel by not engaging in that experience, it has done nothing but make the subject more untouchable. Kansas can move forward by making this topic one of interest, not debate.

I hope to someday experience this trip to the National Historical Site with my class and my history teacher with the chance to just discuss and be able to talk about what Brown v. Board stands for. Another way Kansas can move forward is to establish more museums and historical societies about African American, Native American, and other important ethnicities in American History. The Brown vs. Board Site left such an impact on me and I feel establishing new places of this type would only further my interest in ethnic backgrounds. Finally, Kansas can move forward by keeping the idea of segregation behind us, but keeping the history of segregation right in front of us. The lessons learned, battles won, and the incredible determination that Brown vs. Board provided our state helped Kansas reach "To the Stars" and will continue to do so if we as Kansans utilize the fresh values of our astounding history.

Ultimately, Oliver Brown and the Brown v. Board of Education case remains in the back of my mind, shaping my decisions and forming my morals. Kansas offers many things: sunflower farms, impressive agriculture, and a lot of corn fields, but one thing that stands out to me about Kansas is the diversity, and the acceptance of this diversity. I hold a firm belief that Kansas events like Brown vs. Board shaped the mindsets of Kansans and how we treat one another, so, while we have a lot to learn from this historical event, we already learned so much from it, and it shows. I consider it an advantage living not only in Kansas, but relatively close to Topeka. I often visit this wonderful city to accomplish everyday tasks, but every once in a while, I am free to visit the Brown vs. Board of Education National Historic Site and I am reminded of so many things.

I am reminded that I am lucky and privileged to live with nothing keeping me from achieving my aspirations. I am reminded that I am blessed to live in such a diverse place. I am reminded that with grit and perseverance, I can accomplish all my goals. When I get to walk the streets just north of the capitol building, there is a completely different environment. I can look up at the towering, beautiful French architecture, admire Ad Astra standing firm, facing the bright blue sky, and get reminded all over again of how Kansas history shaped me and that I know I am aiming "To the Stars."

The Dust Bowl
Elsie Fleming
Grade 8
Iola Middle School

It's the year 1931, and you're a wheat farmer in central Kansas. During World War I, you planted acres upon acres of wheat, hoping to make some money from the increased demand, but the wheat prices have plummeted. After harvest you hope to break even. While working one windy day, you see a rising dark cloud in the distance. You run back to your house as the black cloud approaches and cover any cracks with wet rags. You've heard of these before– dust storms. Surrounding states have been experiencing them for the past few months. The sound of billions of particles of dirt hitting your house echos around the room. All you can do is hold your family close and hope for the best.

The 1930's were a challenging time for most Americans due to the Great Depression, but many Kansans (and other people in the Midwest) also had to live through the severe devastation of the Dust Bowl. Nearly 7,000 people died from "dust pneumonia", a condition where the lungs fill with dust. Over 250,000 people fled the plains in search of jobs and a safer environment away from the massive dust storms that covered Kansas. While much of the cause for the storms were do to the severe drought that plagued the entire nation during the 1930s, common agricultural practices also contributed to the severity of the "Dirty Thirties".

During World War I, rising wheat prices led to increased wheat production in Kansas. While this was good for the economy, it was not good for the soil. Farmers furiously plowed their fields, planting as much wheat as possible. When wheat prices eventually plummeted during the Great Depression, the farmers took a financial hit. They scrounged around for any and all ground to plant and harvest wheat- even land unfit for farming- in hopes to at least break even. The cumulative effects of severely dry weather and marginal land caused the crops to fail, leaving huge amounts of dry, barren soil.

During the 1930's, America suffered a severe drought from virtually coast to coast, but the Midwest suffered worst of all. The soil that had been exposed by Kansan farmers while they furiously worked to increase wheat production was now dried to a crisp. High winds blew massive amounts of dust from dozens and dozens of desolate farm lands all the way from Texas to Nebraska. Dust storms had occurred in Kansas' past, but none as severe as as those in the 1930s. This increase in severity was attributed to all the loose soil from the excessive wheat/grain production combined with the excruciating drought.

By 1934, 35 million acres of land in the Midwest was deemed unfit for farming and another 125 million acres was rapidly deteriorating. Thousands became homeless and lost their land to the devastating storms. However, the worst was yet to come.

On April 14, 1935, a black cloud covered over southern Kansas. The storm lasted for hours and stretched from the Oklahoma panhandle to southeastern Colorado. Some people were blinded or inhaled so much dust that "dust pneumonia" was inevitable. An estimated three million tons of soil blew off the Great Plains on the accurately named "Black Sunday". Other horrific storms added to the effects of the Great Depression. The struggle drew to a close as, finally, regular rainfall started back up in 1939.

Despite all of Kansas' hardships, the Dust Bowl did lead to some great advancements in political policy and agricultural technology. For instance, because of the harrowing effects of the storms, President Franklin D. Roosevelt established the Soil Erosion Service (now called the Natural Resources Conservation Service) and the Prairie States Forestry Project in 1935. These projects led to farmers planting trees across the plains to create windbreaks and implementing new farming techniques such as contour plowing. Also, the federal government began paying farmers to take infertile lands out of production, helping to reduce soil losses. Techniques like crop rotation also began being used after the Dust Bowl.

When farmers began to practice these new techniques, soil loss was reduced by 65%. However, there weren't many people left in Kansas after the previous years of hardship. Roughly one-third of people fled Kansas in hopes of a safer and more financially secure environment. Looking back, that might be viewed as a blessing in disguise. The large number of farmers in Kansas contributed to the prairie being over-plowed, which contributed to the Dust Bowl.

Farmers, and anybody in Kansas, have a lot to learn from the events of the Dust Bowl. For one, it proves just how valuable a healthy environment is for us. We literally will not be able to survive if we don't care for our environment, in this particular case, our soil. We depend on the earth to grow materials to build our houses, our food, food for animals that we eat, etc. The Dust Bowl shows us what could happen if we don't care for it properly.

Especially in Kansas, soil health is very important due to our reliance on agriculture for our state economic health. However, even now, farmers use pesticides and fertilizers that are detrimental to soil health because they harm necessary microbes, bacteria, and other essential fauna (e.g. bees). If we're not careful, another Dust Bowl could be in our future. Despite these concerns, there are many good practices that farmers are using, like cover crops and contour plowing. Additionally, Kansas State University is studying new farming techniques and educating farmers through the Kansas State Extension Service network across Kansas.

We always hear about pollution and CO2 emissions, but we rarely hear about soil health. By looking back in the past at the Dust Bowl, we can learn from our mistakes and prevent another series environmental disasters. Kansas exports around $3.6 billion every year in agricultural exports, so if we take a look at our practices and how they're affecting our soil, then maybe we can influence others to do the same.

Works Cited

The Dust Bowl of the 1930s, livinghistoryfarm.org/farminginthe30s/water_02.html.

"Dust Bowl." *Kansas Historical Society*, www.kshs.org/kansapedia/dust-bowl/12040].

Editors, History.com. "Dust Bowl." *History.com*, A&E Television Networks, 27 Oct. 2009, www.history.com/topics/great-depression/dust-bowl.

Greenspan, Jesse. "Remembering Black Sunday, 80 Years Later." *History.com*, A&E Television Networks, 14 Apr. 2015, www.history.com/news/remembering-black-sunday-80-years-later.

"Kansas in the 1930s." *Kansas Historical Society*, www.kshs.org/p/kansas-in-the-1930s/13202.

"What the Dust Bowl Taught Farmers - Ask Farm Aid." *Farm Aid*, 22 July 2015, www.farmaid.org/blog/ask-farm-aid-dust-bowl/.

To The Stars Through Difficulties Together
Josie Gage
Grade 10
Dexter High School

Kansas has drastically improved from a time when there was a major division between the different race and ethnicities of this state. Since then, we have come together as a state and as a people to achieve numerous accomplishments. Multiple historical events have shaped Kansas to become what it is today. There are several events of honorable mention, but none have had as much significance nor as large an impact on our state —let alone on our nation— than the case of *Brown vs. The Board of Education of Topeka*.

The beginnings of what would later be known as the Brown vs. The Board of Education case developed in September of 1950 when Oliver Brown's 7-year-old daughter Linda Brown was denied access to an all-white school based on the precedent that she was black. In order for Brown's daughter to get an education, she had to travel across town to Monroe Elementary, one of four black schools in Topeka. Linda Brown could have instead gone to the all-white Sumner Elementary school, located just four blocks from their home if it were not for her being refused admittance. Not only was the travel distance a great inconvenience, but the quality of education and the condition of the school, both of which were rudimentary at best, were as well due to the lack of funding provided by the state. With Linda Brown's education in jeopardy, Brown would be compelled not only to do something for his daughter, but also for all blacks and their children. This motivated him to file a class-action lawsuit against the Board of Education of Topeka on February 28, 1951.

The Brown vs. Board of Education of Topeka case actually consisted of five cases, which were then combined by the Supreme Court. The other four cases had been based on the alleged discrimination of other parents' children, which resulted in them not being allowed to attend all-white schools in previous years. These cases had been combined because they had all been filed against the Board of Education of Topeka for the segregation of schools. As a result, on December 9, 1952, Robert Carter began his argument and represented the Brown family and other plaintiffs. Assistant Attorney General Paul Wilson represented the state of Kansas in this trial. By the fall of 1952, a group of Topekan school board members had been elected who did not want segregation to continue and wanted to move toward integrating schools. After the oral argument posed by the two parties, the Supreme Court justices remained deeply divided on whether or not to abolish segregation in schools. The Court scheduled a reargument for October 12, 1953, focusing on the original understanding of the Fourteenth Amendment. However, this plan was to change due to unexpected circumstances.

On September 9, 1953, Chief Justice Fred Vinson died of cardiac arrest at the age of 63. Less than one month after his death, Earl Warren took the oath of office to become the new Chief Justice of the United States. New arguments concerning the Brown case were rescheduled for December 7, 1953. The new court date soon rolled around and the fighting began anew. After much debate during the trial, the Supreme Court unanimously ruled that segregated public education violated the Equal Protection Clause of the Fourteenth Amendment therefore making it unconstitutional on May 17, 1954.

Kansans can learn a lot from the historical event that occurred in this case which spanned from September of 1950 to May 17, 1954. This case brings to light the flaws of our society. It should serve as an example to the people of Kansas and remind us that we need to move on from a mindset that says we can classify people based on the color of their skin. There are two important lessons that we should commit to memory from the Brown vs. The Board of Education case. Lesson one: we are one people, no matter the shade of our skin. Lesson two: discrimination is unacceptable and everyone deserves the same opportunities, no matter who they may be.

The Kansas school system has not completely eradicated discrimination in schools. Many children and young adults are still bullied and have hate crimes committed against them due to the color of their skin. It is a problem that Kansas and the nation acknowledge and are constantly trying to alleviate. However, we have made much progress and will continue to do so as we are fueled by the need for change. The U.S. Department of Education reports that since the *Brown vs. The Board of Education of Topeka* case, there has been a 5.0 to 9.9 percent increase of the enrollment of minority races in public elementary and secondary schools nationwide. As of 2018, African Americans make up 6.2% of students enrolled in public schools and Hispanics and Latinos make up another 11.9% of those students. Minority races now make up 25.5 percent of all students present in public schools all across the United States. This data is proof that we are gradually improving Kansas's education system. We can only hope that we can set an example for generations to come and maintain this trend.

It seems like every day we see in mainstream media some type of racist activity or crime has taken place in Kansas or somewhere in our nation. The media portrays to watchers that we are all bad people that are out to hurt each other just because we look different. This is a lie. Not every black person is a gangster, not every white person is a supremacist. People of different color and backgrounds do get along with each other. Some of us become friends, some of us become families, and most of us respect one another. We say hello to passersby, give hugs and high-fives, we open doors for the young, old, black, and white — things that have become part of our everyday lives. This is our society now, and it should continue to be this way no matter who or what influences us to be different.

We need to go forward from this point and learn to respect, love, and fairly treat one another. We especially need to learn from our children because they are the new generation and will decide how the world will be. I believe they have often been on the right path, but have been led astray by their parents and the influences of others and then proceeded to mislead their own children. They always treat everyone fairly and do not care what another child looks like, as long as they will be their friend. That is how we should treat others every single day. We should be willing to spend time with those who look like us and those who don't. We should being willing to help when someone falls and be there to pick them back up again. We should be willing to love one another as God always intended for us to.

Every Kansan should take a close look at the *Brown vs. The Board of Education of Topeka* case and remember what it did for our state and for our nation. It bound us together as a people that would go on to give everyone, no matter what they looked like, the same opportunities as everyone else. As we continue with our daily lives, we will encounter many challenges that we will easily conquer if we stand together. When that time comes, we need to look back on this historical event and remember our state motto: Ad astra per aspera. The people of Kansas need to know that we are the state it is today because we have been to the stars through difficulties together.

Prohibition—And the Lessons It Should Have Taught
Dan Hardy
Grade 11
Nickerson High School

As we have been instructed, Kansas does indeed have a long and rich history. Further, it is true that in any such rich history, there must be a mixture of both positive and negative events—fortunate and unfortunate happenings. It is my contention that prohibition, one of the events often mentioned in any listing of important Kansas happenings, was certainly one of the more unfortunate episodes to mar the Kansas historical timeline.

Kansas, seen by many as seldom being a pioneer in new and modern ideologies sweeping our nation, was indeed the first state to pass a constitutional amendment prohibiting the manufacture or sales of intoxicating beverages. The Kansas Prohibitory Law was adopted by a popular vote of the people in November 1880 and became effective on May 1, 1882. The many Kansas temperance societies had been highly successful in convincing the legislature and the people that through temperance Kansas could achieve a level of respectability and calm unknown throughout her tumultuous early years. Throughout the early years of Kansas Prohibition, several renowned national figures went on record as favoring the practice of prohibition. In late 1917, General Leonard Wood, then the commanding officer at Fort Riley announced that the Kansas recruits were out performing their peers from other states. "These Kansas boys were brought up in a clean atmosphere--they started right, " Wood told then Kansas Governor Capper. "You can tell the Kansas people for me that they have got the finest, the cleanest, the healthiest and the most vigorous soldiers in point of endurance we have ever seen. The official records show this". (Bader 203) The rest of the nation watched and wondered. Could Kansas' "noble experiment" --a term coined by President Herbert Hoover (History 2019) --really do as Kansans claimed and reduce crime and corruption, solve social problems, reduce the tax burdens of the poor and criminal, and improve the health and hygiene of all people? Even in the face of such noble claims many had doubts and the nation as a whole did not join the ranks of prohibition for another three decades. With the passage of the Eighteenth Amendment to the constitution, on January 29, 1920 the manufacture, sale, or transportation of intoxicating liquors, or the importing or exporting of such liquors, became illegal throughout the United States and all of her territories. Prohibition had come to the United States and conservative Kansas had led the way!

One of the first outcomes from prohibition to be noticed across America was the loss in revenue and taxes from liquor sales and manufacturing. In addition, nearly every jurisdiction in the country felt an increase in governmental spending as they tried to control the illegal alcohol trade, often overseen by members of various organized crime groups. In Kansas, where those who opposed Prohibition already had nearly two decades of practice in the illegal manufacture and sales of liquor, local and outside bootlegging and other efforts to thwart the law were rampant. Some historians credit the influx of big city mobsters and crime families into the urban areas of Wichita and Kansas City as giving rise to the gangs that still plague those areas today. In addition to those who came from outside of Kansas to profit from the illegal trade, there were no shortage of Kansans who were willing to join the bootleg industry. As time passed the Kansas people, as well as other Americans, were becoming increasingly tolerant of the frequent reports of liquor law violations. Even a huge liquor bust like that of May 12, 1930 in Reno and Sedgwick counties-- that collected six giant five hundred gallon stills, seven distribution depots, tons of sugar, six thousand gallons of quality sugar whiskey valued at sixty thousand dollars wholesale, and a denatured alcohol stripping plant-in all a half a million dollar liquor operation did little to rouse the interest of a people now facing the much larger crisis of a deepening national depression. (Bader 201) With the coming of the Great Depression, American dependency on alcohol rose. With no readily available outlets for commercial alcohol Americans turned to less safe substances and sources. The instances of poisoning and death increased. Crimes rates rose and prison systems were stretched to their maximum capacity. Corruption was rampant. All of this, and there were no measurable gains being made--in fact American alcohol consumption rose during Prohibition. Over time Americans came to see just how unenforceable and negative Prohibition really was, and a movement to repeal the 18th Amendment eventually gave rise to the 21st Amendment to the United States Constitution which would end Prohibition on the national level, while leaving the individual states and other jurisdictions, like counties and cities, with a local option to keep all or part of the liquor prohibitions in place. The Amendment was ratified and became law on December 5, 1933 when Utah became the thirty-sixth state to vote for ratification, giving the Amendment the requisite three-fourths majority needed. The passage of the 21st Amendment did not mean an immediate end to Prohibition in Kansas, however. In fact, Kansas has never ratified the 21st Amendment. Statewide Prohibition lingered on in Kansas until 1948--giving Kansas the distinction of having of having the longest tenure of Prohibition of any state in the Union.

Even though Statewide Prohibition ended in 1948, liquor-by-the drink was still largely controlled until 1987. Three western Kansas counties remain dry yet now. (History)

This information is important to my paper because it demonstrates the level of tenacity with which some Kansans are determined to hold onto a concept, even after the vast majority of the American populace has come to realize the idea is without tangible merit. For Kansas to ever rise to take her true place among the stars, the Kansas people must shed their antiquated conservatism and their religious zeal to legislate and control the morality of others. The lessons that should have been learned from Prohibition still maintain importance today. As Kansas moves forward to face the issues of today--the war on drugs; the need to reduce American dependence on tobacco; the burning questions on censorship and gambling, and hot button topics like abortion--she must accept the evidence which shows that the prohibiting of even marginally mutually beneficial exchanges is sure to fail. This is simple economic law. No matter how much we may all want to help our brothers overcome their bad habits-the creation of an underground market for these personal vices will never solve the problem. Instead, we must stand tall, admit to our issues, and work openly to address the problems they cause. Only by being open and honestly welcoming, personally and economically, can Kansas hope to attain her true greatness and move upward to the stars!.

Works Cited

Bader, Robert Smith. *Prohibition in Kansas: a History*. University Press of Kansas/Eurospan, 1987.

Peak, Kenneth J., and Patricia A. Peak. *Kansas Temperance: Much Ado about Booze*, 1870-1920. Sunflower University

Press, 2000.

Thornton, Mark. https://www.cato.org/publications/policy-analysis/alcohol prohibition-was-failure, 1991

18th and 21st Amendments. https://www.history.com/topics/united-states constitution/18th-and-21st-amendments, 2019

The Dust Bowl
Bailey Jackson
Grade 7
Liberty Middle School

We Kansans have gone through many hard things before in life. I believe though that the most important event that has occurred in our history was The Dust Bowl of the 1930's. The dust storms that were raging through the midwest were what people called "black blizzards". They swirled through Kansas, Oklahoma, Texas, and kept going through other states. These dust storms caused numerous terrible things to happen.

That is why I have decided to share this with you today. I believe that Kansans can learn from The Dust Bowl and it can help our state move forward by doing crop rotation every year, using our tractors smartly, and by not growing any more crops than we need.

The first reason on why I thought The Dust Bowl would help Kansans move forward is by doing crop rotation every year. By doing crop rotation we can keep the soil healthy, we can have a higher yield, and it will help rule out all the weeds. If we keep the soil healthy, we could keep growing our own food. We could also have a higher yield if we switched our crops every year. By doing so, we might even make a better profit.

Another reason on why doing crop rotation is valuable, is because of all the weeds we could eliminate from our crops for the year. We could do crop rotation every year and it would help us keep out some of the plants we do not need in our crops, and it might not harm them like some of the weed killers we use. Most weed killers are not healthy for us to eat or healthy for the crops we are growing.

My next reason on why I thought The Dust Bowl would

help Kansans move forward is by using our tractors smartly. During The Dust Bowl, people were using their tractors day and night to plow fields and it was making all the topsoil extremely loose. Since the Midwest was in a drought, that made all of the topsoil dry and exceedingly hard to plant their crops. It did not take long for the wind to pick up, thus causing the big dust storm. I believe that us Kansans can learn from this by not using our tractors all day and night to plow the fields.

My last reason on why I believe Kansans can learn from the aftermath and move forward from The Dust Bowl is by not growing any more crops than we need. During The Dust Bowl, they favored how valuable the wheat was and kept planting it. This caused a great deal of time on the tractor which caused even more topsoil to loosen up. With all of the top soil loose, this again allowed the wind to pick up the excess soil and be blown away. As American farmers, we need to be careful on not being greedy and not growing any more than we need, especially with the farming equipment we have today. I definitely think Kansans can learn from this.

In conclusion, I believe that Kansans could learn and move forward from The Dust Bowl because of all the terrible things that have happened. I can conclude that we can move forward from what we can and have learned about this time period. I believe that Kansans can learn from The Dust Bowl and it will help our state move forward by doing crop rotation every year, using our tractors smartly, and not growing any more crops than we need.

"The storm took place at sundown; it lasted through the night. When we looked out next morning, we saw a terrible sight. We saw outside our window where wheat fields they had grown. Was now a rippling ocean of dust the wind had blown." by Woody Guthrie, The Great Dust Storm. While all of the atrocious events that happened in the 1930's, we still all have a lesson to learn. We can all learn to not be greedy about what we already have in front of us, but to remember to stay smart and learn from other people's' mistakes. If we can help it, we do not want to repeat history in an unacceptable way on account of how much I love living and growing up on a Kansas farm and could not bear to imagine what it would be like if I had to live that way or any other way.

The Kansas-Nebraska Act
Grace Elizabeth Johnson
Grade 5
Mission Valley Elementary

About the Kansas-Nebraska Act

The Kansas-Nebraska Act was passed by the U.S. Congress on May 30, 1854.

The Act allowed people in Kansas and Nebraska territories to decide for themselves whether or not to allow slavery within their borders. The Act infuriated many people in the North, who considered the Missouri Compromise to be a binding agreement. After the Act was passed, pro and anti-slavery supporters hurriedly settled in Kansas to affect the outcome of the first election held there after the law came into effect.

Pro-slavery settlers carried the election, but they were charged with fraud by anti-slavery settlers. Anti-slavery settlers held another election, but the pro-slavery settlers refused to vote. This caused the establishment of two opposing legislatures within Kansas territory. Violence erupted, with the anti-slavery settlers led by John Brown. The territory earned the nickname "Bleeding Kansas".

Franklin Pierce, the 14th president, was in support of the pro-slavery settlers, and sent in Federal troops to stop violence and disperse the anti-slavery legislature. Another election was called. Again, pro-slavery settlers won and, again, they were charged with fraud. As a result, Congress did not recognize the constitution adopted by the pro-slavery settlers and Kansas was not allowed to become a state. Eventually, anti-slavery settlers outnumbered pro-slavery settlers and a new constitution was drawn up. On January 29, 1861, right before the start of the Civil War, Kansas was admitted to the union as a free state.

What We Can Learn from This Event

What I think Kansans can learn from this event is that even though we had fought for a long time, I think we ended up making the right decision. Even though the pro-slavery settlers won twice, the anti-slavery settlers kept fighting, and eventually, they outnumbered the pro-slavery settlers, and now, there isn't slavery in Kansas. This can teach Kansans to never give up and keep fighting for what you believe in. I think this is a very inspiring story and a lot of people can learn from it. This is the first time I have learned about the Kansas-Nebraska Act, and it has already inspired me so much. When I think about how many people can learn from it, especially pro-slavery supporters, it amazes me. It is so cool that Kansas was a part of this and so many people actually help slavery be banned in Kansas.

THANK YOU

Brown Versus Ferguson: The Case for Desegregation
Chase Kellogg
Grade 12
Riverton High School

Our state of Kansas, and the United States as a whole, was changed forever in 1954 with The Supreme Court ruling on Brown vs. Board of Education. When The Supreme Court unanimously ruled that racial segregation in schools was unconstitutional, it set the stage for a new era of civil rights that would eventually lead to the desegregation of schools across the nation. As well as being a huge step in the direction of a united and tolerant future, the Brown case lit a fuse that would burn down the Plessy v. Ferguson ruling, which had enabled nearly sixty years of unchecked racism. Without the efforts of a group of Kansas families standing up to protest an unjust school system, the freedom and equality we celebrate today may never have come to fruition; this is why I chose Brown versus the Board of Education as the topic for my Kansas historical essay.

Although Brown versus the Board of Education gained national fame for its status as a landmark supreme court case, it began much closer to home. It began as a class action lawsuit against the Board of Education of the City of Topeka, Kansas. In 1951, a group consisting of thirteen African-American parents, representing their twenty respective children, called for a suit against the board of education due to the inequality in schooling provided for minority children. An 1879 law permitted racial segregation for blacks and whites in the Kansas school districts, but did not require it, providing a legal premise for the plaintiffs of Brown. Many of the parents involved in the suit had been recruited by members of the NAACP

(National Association for the Advancement of Colored People), in an attempt to strike out against the longstanding racial segregation in Kansas schools. An African-American man named Oliver Brown was chosen to be the named plaintiff in the case. His daughter, Linda Carol, was a third grade student who, every day, had to take mile long bus ride to get to her segregated school, while a white only school stood just seven blocks from her house. To provide a basis for the case, the parents recruited for Brown were all instructed to enroll their children in the white only school nearest to their homes, and were each subsequently denied. Following this, the parents collectively filed suit, and the case was taken before the District Court. Unsurprisingly, the court ruled against the plaintiffs, citing Plessy v. Ferguson as a just cause for the board's standard of 'separate but equal.' Following an appeal, Brown proceeded to the level of The Supreme Court, and was combined with a number of other similar cases, collectively referred to as Brown vs. Board of Education. Brown was represented by Thurgood Marshall, who would later serve as the first African-American justice on The Supreme Court. The case was initially heard in the spring of 1953, but the court remained undecided and requested to rehear the case that fall. On the 17th of May, 1954, the United States Supreme Court made its final vote on the matter of Brown vs. Board of Education, unanimously ruling in favor of Brown. The court had found through a number of psychological examinations that segregation caused black children to feel inferior and prevented them from achieving their full potential. They came to the ultimate conclusion that separate but equal is inherently unequal, and therefore deprive of the 14th Amendment's equal protection clause. The Supreme Court's verdict in the case of Brown vs. Board of Education helped to strike a nail into the coffin of Plessy vs. Ferguson, and pave the pathway for the modern era of equal rights.

While Brown v. Board of Education was a landmark case that shaped the United States as a whole, it had a very specific and personal impact for the citizens of Kansas. Ever since The Supreme Court announced its final verdict fifty-five years ago, segregation and racial tensions in Kansas have never been the same. When our state was first born in the 1850's, a great and bloody war was waged over whether or not slavery should be permitted within our borders. In the end of that conflict, Kansas emerged as a free state, setting us on a path to freedom and justice for men and women of every skin color. But, when the ruling of Plessy v. Ferguson was decided in 1896, a symbolic log was placed in the roadway to civil rights. Without a few resilient Kansas parents who chose to stand up for their children's freedoms, our state may have lingered for many years in doubt and self-delusion concerning issues of segregation and discrimination. I believe that Kansans can learn a great deal from Brown v. Board of Education, and I believe that we should continue to teach our students about our rich history and the powerful forces that united us.

The case of Brown was a many sided story, with each individual's experience in the matter being quite different from the next. But all of them learned something very important from it, and so can we. Brown shows Kansans that no matter who someone is, no matter where someone came from, they can change the future by bravely standing up for what's right, even in the face of indeterminable odds. Another important truth this case taught us is that unification is stronger than segregation. During the time of the Brown case, many of the African-American citizens of our state wanted equal education and better schooling for their children, but not necessarily an end to segregation; for many of them, having their children separated from white students was not just a curse, but a blessing as well. The era of racial intolerance stemmed from both sides, and many citizens of either skin color desired to remain separated. For the parents of Brown however, it was more important to stand up for a unifying cause rather than remain divided for petty disdain. Their actions proved once again to the country, and to our state, that justice can prevail if fought for.

I believe this case should remain as a beacon for the state of Kansas, a point from which we can continue on the right path. Now that schools are unsegregated, we should focus on working together in the American spirit of freedom and individuality, regardless of skin color. The parents who fought for their children were also fighting for a future very similar to the one that Dr. King famously dreamed in 1963; a future where people are judged by the content of their character rather than the color of their skin. Brown was an enormous first step toward achieving this, and therefore it shouldn't be left as just another piece of forgotten history, irrelevant to the majority of our citizens; it should be held onto as a light pointing in the direction of the future we want for our state and nation. Instead of focusing on the pain and suffering caused by cases like Plessy v. Ferguson and the Jim Crow laws, we should teach our students how we overcame those atrocities, and thus teach them to continue overcoming in that same spirit of freedom.

In conclusion, I chose Brown vs. Board of Education because it represents a major fight for justice that our state won. And it wasn't the government or the administration who won it, but the people. Brown shows us that we can move forward, we can stand for liberty, and we can be brave in our fight for freedom. Without the case of Brown, much of our happier days in history would not have been as bright for our citizens. For the past one hundred and forty-eight years, Kansans have been fighting tyranny and riding on towards freedom, and Brown will forever stand as a golden chapter in that story.

Works Cited

"Black, White, and Brown." Online NewsHour: Brown v. Board of Education -- May 12, 2004, Online NewsHour, 12 May 2004, web.archive.org/web/20040610182739/http://www.pbs.org/newshour/bb/law/jan-june04/brown_05-12.html#.

Cottrol, Robert J. "Brown v. Board of Education." Brown v. Board of Education - Federalism in America, Center for the Study of Federalism, 2006, encyclopedia.federalism.org/index.php/Brown_v._Board_of_Education.

Finkelman, Paul. "Brown v. Board of Education of Topeka." WebCite Query Result, Microsoft® Encarta® Online Encyclopedia 2009, 1997, www.webcitation.org/5kwQQveNZ?url=http://encarta.msn.com/encyclopedia_761588641/brow n_v_board_of_cducation_of_topeka.html.

Woo, Elaine. "Kenneth Clark, 90; His Studies Influenced Ban on Segregation." Los Angeles Times, Los Angeles Times, 3 May 2005, www.latimes.com/archives/la-xpm-2005-may-03-me-clark3-story.html.

To the Stars Through the Greatest of Difficulties
Lily Kuhn
Grade 10
Spring Hill High School

The United States of America bled during the Civil War; 600,000 lives were lost and the union was permanently fractured. States turned against each other, turning neighbor against neighbor as war spread its diseased fingers through the nation. Kansas, a young territory, was suddenly the center of conflict as countless outsiders debated over its place in the nation. From Missouri and other states, thousands of people flooded the territory to fight and illegally vote. John Brown, an abolitionist from the East, came to Kansas to fight militant pro-slavery forces. Kansas was in a tumultuous territory in a tumultuous time, and under siege in a thousand different ways. Yet, the citizens of the territory pulled through, founding a state which could enter the union holding freedom for all who came.

The legality of slavery in the United States had been carefully balanced by several complex compromises and deals that guaranteed the number of free-states and slave-states remained equal. The nation, however, continued to expand despite such delicate dealings. The Kansas-Nebraska Act created the new territories Nebraska and Kansas from previously unorganized Native American lands. The Missouri Compromise forced all territories north of a certain latitude to be free-states, so Congress split the land into two territories to avoid upsetting the balance of states. Furthermore, it was decided that each territory would vote on the legality of slavery in each respective state. The settlers of Nebraska were correctly assumed to be largely anti-slavery, and slavery was prohibited in the territory without much bother. Kansas was similarly assumed, due to its more southern geography and proximity to Missouri, to be solidly pro-slavery, which would maintain the balance of states. However, it soon became clear that Congress had vastly underestimated the abolitionist resistance in the territory. What was presumed to be a quick solution soon devolved into a vicious battle for Kansas's soul.

Immigrants from across the nation flooded the territory, each desperate to make their voice heard in the great debate. Many on both sides set up residency in Kansas to gain the right to vote in its elections, but still more had nefarious purposes in the territory. Pro-slavery factions would use various methods, like fraud and intimidation, to win elections, and Border-Ruffians poured in from Missouri to sway elections. These armed, pro-slavery outlaws corrupted many early elections in the territory; in one case, there were 1,729 fraudulent votes in an election, compared to only 1,114 legal votes. Abolitionist forces moved in on the territory, as well. These "Free-Staters" came from Northern states, and were often funded and supplied by organizations from back East. Those who made such efforts included Henry Ward Beecher, who became known for "Beecher's Bibles," rifles that were labeled as bibles in the wooden crates that were used to send them to the Free-Staters in Kansas. Each side was growing bolder in its fight, and all out war seemed more inevitable with each passing day.

The election for Kansas's first territorial legislature took place on March 30, 1855, and would determine whether the territory would become a free-state or not. Border Ruffians once more flooded the state from Missouri to illegally vote in the election, and the territory came away from the election with 37 of 39 seats of the legislature filled with pro-slavery delegates. The results of five voting districts were invalidated by the territorial governor and were replaced by the results of a special election, but at the end the pro-slavery factions held strong with 29 seats. Tensions rose in the fragile territorial government, and few trusted the disputed results of the elections. After investigating the territory's elections, Congress determined that had there been no interference by illegal voting, Kansas would have elected a Free-State legislature and that the current legislature was an illegal body. However, the pro-slavery legislature seized control and began forming laws that enforced slavery in the territory. In response, abolitionist and anti-slavery residents formed their own legislature, which was rejected by President Franklin Pierce's pro-slavery administration. Under rule by two governments, the territory was quickly descending into chaos, and tensions were reaching a boiling point.

At that point, violence was nigh inevitable. In early 1865, the abolitionist town of Lawrence was raided and ransacked by pro-slavery Missourians and Kansas settlers, led by Douglas County Sheriff Samuel J. Jones. Though there was only one fatality in the conflict, several buildings in the town were destroyed, including the Free State Hotel and the home of the state's first governor, Charles L. Robinson. Unknown at the time, the event seems to foreshadow the coming Lawrence Massacre, in which 164 Lawrence civilians were murdered by Confederate William Quantrill and his forces. However, it was the first sacking of Lawrence that sparked the guerrilla warfare in Bleeding Kansas. After the sacking, abolitionist John Brown and his sons seized five men from the pro-slavery settlement at Pottawatomie Creek. Brown and his sons killed the men with broadswords, sparking controversy even in abolitionist groups with their brutality. Guerrilla violence continued for years afterward and throughout the duration of the Civil War. Afterward, the long battle between the two groups appeared impossible to forget.

Today, the legacy of Bleeding Kansas remains as familiar as any other facet of our history. The struggle between Kansas and Missouri has never disappeared, despite all efforts; even now, the Kansas Jayhawks and the Missouri Tigers maintain a bitter rivalry, and the states bitterly argue over the superior Kansas City. However, there is a reason every child in Kansas is eventually taught about Bleeding Kansas. Despite the terrors and uncertainty of the time, always surrounded by violence and unstable governments, the people of Kansas persevered. Early Kansans led the nation toward a more noble path, one without slavery and injustice. Together, despite every obstacle, they built a state that could survive its turbulent origins and find its way out of the dark and to the stars.

Wind Energy in Kansas
Cashlyn Kvasnicka
Grade 8
Quinter Junior Senior High School

Wind has been associated specifically with Kansas as long as we've been a state. From tumbling tumbleweeds, to the Dust Bowl, and even to the tornado in The Wizard of Oz... the wind is more than blowing currents of air to Kansas; it's an event. It's an event that occurs almost daily; in fact, days with no wind are rare in our great state. This predictable behavior, though used through windmills for pumping water or in mills for grinding grain, forcefully takes on a more useful purpose: generating power for Kansas and its future.

In the 1800's, farmers and ranchers decided to take advantage of the wind and start working with it instead of against it. Inventors, farmers, and ranchers created what is called a "windmill". Windmills are machines that use the wind to create energy and put it to work. They used the windmill for pumping water for their crops, animals, and daily living needs. These machines were also used for grinding grain, cutting wood in saw mills and creating paper in paper mills. The windmill was modified with new technology to create wind turbines that you can see popping up throughout the Kansas prairies.

Much like a meeting of like-minded people all collectively joined for one common purpose, the wind turbines located throughout parts of Kansas also work together for the purpose to generate power. As one travels along highways throughout Kansas, the ever increasing numbers of wind farms cannot go unnoticed. The large blades of these turbines begin storing the tremendous untapped potential of the wind. Currently, Kansas possesses over 20 wind farms, with the largest one (named

Smoky Hills) located in Ellsworth and Lincoln counties with over 100 owners. These owners get paid an average $8,000 dollars a year. Wind farms are being developed all over the state, with the newest wind farm south of Colby running east and west of I-70.

Wind turbines are becoming such a huge deal to Kansas. Even though the weather can be unpredictable and at times annoying, this phenomenon does serve a useful purpose. The wind is being used in more useful ways than ever. Universities like Fort Hays State University are utilizing wind power for its own wind farms to generate power for over half of the campus. It saves the campus over $500,000 dollars a year on energy costs.

Wind turbines can be a way to help save the environment by generating wind power to create no emissions since they require no fossil fuels to function. More importantly, these turbines are utilizing a renewable resource. Wind power continues to be a fast-growing industry to battle the use of fossil fuels. Wind turbine farms in Kansas have seen terrific growth, and wind farms are continually going up all over Kansas. Much of the growth and popularity stems from the boost to the local economy in areas like mine in Northwest Kansas.

The winds of Kansas have blown for centuries, creating scenes of tumbling tumbleweeds, dust storms crossing fields, and windmills spinning on the prairie. The winds of Kansas have recently boosted growth and popularity of wind turbine farms. This shift in energy use not only boosts local economies, but it also generates power without using fossil fuels. Though wind will always be a part of our state's past and present, it's the promising future use of wind that places Kansas at the front of the winds of change.

To the Stars Through Student Voice and Choice
Callie Locke
Grade 7
South Haven Junior High School

There are very many important events in Kansas history, one event was when the box turtle became the state reptile (Ornate Box Turtle). This was a very important event in Kansas because the Caldwell students showed that every human has a voice and every voice is important; every human should know that! If all students know that, they can speak up now and they can help this state be the best this state can possibly be.

A class from Caldwell has nominated the Box Turtle to be the state reptile. On April fourteenth, 1989 the Box turtle became the state reptile. Then governor John Carlin signed the bill to have a new state reptile, the box turtle! The teacher at the time was Mr. Larry Miller and the principal at the time was Mr. Lewis Stookey. The sixth grade students had carried around an Ornate Box Turtle named Tina when they traveled around the state to promote their cause. The students in sixth grade sent letters to the state capital to nominate the Box Turtle. These students showed that everyone in this universe has a voice that needs to be heard and everyone has a voice that is so special they should always use it.
Everyone can learn from this so that they all have a voice which should be heard, no matter what. Currently, there is a movement in Kansas called Student voice and choice.

Teachers want students to use their voices because they can give their teachers and administrators feedback about their day, good or bad help students' school day be the best it can be.

This student voice, student choice practice can help everyone in so many ways. One example is when the sixth graders in Caldwell voiced that the box turtle should become the state reptile. The youth of Kansas will be running the state in a few years. The students in this state need to learn that they have a voice, now, because some adults don' t always remember that. If the students start using their voices now, they can learn to speak up and help Kansas raise our future leaders and continue doing great things.

There are so many very important events in Kansas history, just like the Box Turtle becoming the Kansas state reptile. Students voice is so valuable. Students need to always be aware of that, and never let anyone change that. No voice or idea can be replaced! If some students start speaking up now, when they get older they can help this state be the best it possibly can be.

Works Cited

Caldwell, Kansas 67022, tcslacerta.tripod.com/tcsphotos /id 1 3.html. "Ornate Box Turtle." *Kansas Historical Society*, www.kshs.org/kansapedia/omate-box-tu rtle/17237. "Student Voice & Choice." *ReDesign*, www.redesignu.org/design-lab/mastery-learning/resource-bank/student-voice-choice. "Student Voice and Student Choice: The 21st Century Approach to Teaching and Learning."

Milton Hershey School, www.mhsstudents.org/student-voice-student-choice/.

Amelia Earhart
Amelia Marten
Grade 5
Garden Plain Elementary

A historical event that happened in Kansas was that Amelia Earhart was born in Atchison, Kansas. She was the sixteenth woman to be given a pilot's license in 1923. As a ten-year-old girl, she had her first plane ride in California in December, 1920. She was flown by the veteran Frank Hawks. When she got off the plane she exclaimed, "As soon as I left the ground, I knew I had to be the one to fly."

Kansans can learn from Earhart because she showed us that no matter what, we should still push for our goals. She was pushed back from her dreams because women were expected to stay home and let their husbands and sons do all the work. They had to wear long skirts and cheer on males in sports. At the time, flying was only for men; women were scorned when they tried. Amelia did not like how the women gave in to these rules. Even as a child, she tended to act like a tomboy. Another example of a challenge she faced was that her father, Samuel Stanton Earhart, was a drunk. He used to spend almost all of the family's money on drinks. So, when Amelia was taking flight lessons, she had to work to pay for the lessons. Also, when she was saving up to buy her airplane, Amelia worked very hard to save up the money to buy it. Her mother helped her because her father spent a ton of money on his drinks, like I said before. When Amelia and her mother had enough money, Amelia bought a second-hand Kinner Airster biplane that was bright yellow. She called it "The Canary".

Amelia accomplished the goals she had set for herself, just like every Kansan should. Amelia Earhart can help us move forward because she might help people realize how much they can accomplish by pushing for their dream.

I chose Amelia Earhart because my name is Amelia and my dad and I are very passionate about aviation.

https://airandspace.si.edu/explore-and-learn/topics/women-in-aviation/earhart.cfm

https://www.kibin.com/essay-examples/the-different-challenges-of-amelia-earhart-in-life-2NMHFHCn

Brown v. Board of Education
Yu'Nique Reed
Grade 5
Magnet School at Allen

Some states in the U.S. did not have segregation because it was against their laws. But other states, like Kansas, had segregation. Segregation was a very big issue in the 1940s and 1950s. It meant that African Americans and Caucasians were separate in almost everything they did. For example, this meant African Americans were not able to eat in some restaurants, were not able to sit wherever they wanted, and African American kids and Caucasian kids could not go to school together.

Reverend Oliver Brown and his wife wanted their daughter Linda Brown to start third grade at a school close to her house. She had to walk six blocks and across busy train tracks to get to her school bus, which was a 30 minute ride from her segregated school. Her father tried to enroll Linda at the Sumner School, which was for white children only. Sadly, they would not let her in because of the color of her skin. That is why the NAACP (National Association for the Advancement of Colored People) decided to recruit Rev. Brown's family to join twelve other families that had similar problems. The children in all these families had to take unsafe routes and long trips to get to their segregated schools. The goal of the NAACP was to make sure that African Americans and Caucasians were treated equally in all things.

The first case in the Kansas court did not end well for the NAACP. The school board won the case. So the families decided to take a bigger step, to take the case to the Supreme Court. Many people did not care that African Americans and Caucasians had separate schools, based on the law of "separate but equal." In 1896 the Supreme Court decided that if African Americans and Caucasians went to different schools that had equal teachers and buildings, and provided the same learning tools, then it was okay to be separate. The NAACP said even though the schools may be the same, the students felt they were not being treated equally, because they couldn't go to the schools closest to their house. They wanted to keep every child safe and well educated. They argued segregation was wrong because it made African American children feel they were not as great as Caucasian children.

The Chief Justice of the Supreme Court, Fred Vinson, was afraid the case would start a riot and change the country if they said yes to integrating schools. So he decided to put the case on hold. Then he died. President Eisenhower replaced him with Earl Warren. He thought segregation was wrong. When they voted on the case in 1954, the vote was 9-0 for school integration. Justice Warren said, "In the field of public education, the doctrine of "separate but equal" has no place. Separate educational facilities are inherently unequal.""

The impact of Brown v. Board of Education was that African American and Caucasian kids who were playmates got to go to school together and play with each other at recess. It meant that African American children felt equal to Caucasian children. The integrated schools helped inspire other cases that had to do with segregation. It even helped inspire the Montgomery Bus Boycott, which was just a year later.

It is the 65th anniversary of the Supreme Court ruling that desegregated schools. What we can learn from this today is that even though things get difficult, you should not give up on what you think is right. The NAACP could have given up when they lost the case in the Kansas court when they said no to integrating schools. They could have given up when the

Supreme Court put the case on hold. But they felt strongly that children should not have to be unsafe or go long distances to go to school.

When things are unfair, you should work hard for change. For example, when workers are not getting paid enough or treated fairly they can take action and go on strike. In Brown v. Board of Education, the parents and the NAACP took action to make the change they wanted to see happen. They made a case for it and did not give up. They felt they had strong arguments that all children should be together and not be separated by the color of their skin. This case teaches Kansans that kids and their parents have the right to choose to go to a school near them where they can get a good education.

How We Can Make Our Schools Equal
Bailey Scott
Grade 5
Scott Academy

All children are a potential shining star and can change the world through their academic success but cannot do this unless they are treated with fairness. In 1954, the U.S Supreme Court handed down a ruling on Brown vs. The Board of Education. The court ruled that separate but equal is not equal under the 14th Amendment. Linda Brown from Topeka, Kansas wanted to go to the closest school to her but as the school was an all-white school Linda and her sister were forced to go to the all-black school one hour away. Due to this clear inequity the attorneys argued for the first time that the sociological impact was just as important as the physical properties such as teachers, curriculums and books. According to the Supreme Court even though the white and black schools were physically equal, segregation based on race left a potentially permanent feeling of inferiority.

Clearly, the equality in physical and emotional factors played a part in the U.S Supreme Court`s decision. In the Kansas City Metro, families have three choices of education, public school, private school and homeschooling. Family income determines where you can live and where you live determines what public school your kids will go to. While private school and homeschool families' education are determined based on family funds; public schools depend almost exclusively on tax dollars. More tax dollars go to schools in wealthier neighborhoods, with fewer funds for schools in poorer neighborhoods. No tax money is supplied to kids in private schools or to homeschool families. Wealthier schools and poorer schools no matter which option one chooses differ on what is provided physically such as; extra-curricular activities, books, curriculums and equipment such as tablets. Better equipment, curriculum and opportunities are available for wealthier kids whether in public school, private school or homeschool. Obviously, an unequal gap exists with physical needs that did not exist before.

No matter what educational option you choose; your education is limited by the amount of funds available for each student. As students get older they become aware of what curriculums, activities and equipment are available for each student and if their books and curriculums are the best. If they are not the best the kids will feel inferior because they wish they have the same opportunities that the wealthier schools have. The student's emotions play a big part in their academic success. If kids feel inferior their grades will suffer which will hurt them in their academic lives. We can change that by making our schools equal.

Making our schools equal is one of the best ways to help our state move forward. Where once all schools used to be equal at least in physical features, it is obvious that this is no longer the case. We have in fact widened the inequality gap by allowing the schools to be unequal in both physical and emotional factors. If we can give all students the same opportunities our schools will finally be equal. Prior to 1954 the black students felt inferior to the white students just like today the kids at a poor school will feel inferior to the kids at a wealthier school. If we can equal out our schools funding we will have balanced out our school system which will be a wonderful thing for our state to help it move forward. The best way to do this is by giving each child a certain amount of money that stays with them no matter what educational option they choose. This would help balance out the opportunities available for each student and improve the mindsets of poor kids and their families while allowing all children to shine.

A Decade to Learn From
Fiona Stevenson
Grade 5
Tecumseh South Elementary School

I think Kansans are stubborn, friendly, down-to-earth people. We were stubborn enough to join the Union as a free state, even though our neighbors in Missouri tried to change our minds. We are friendly and curious when we meet people from other places with different experiences. When I say that we are down-to-earth, I'm talking about how we are still very much an agricultural state. Once upon a time, our agricultural way of life was threatened. It was a time known as The Dust Bowl. The Dust Bowl began in the early 1930's when a gigantic drought hit a lot of Midwestern states, including Kansas. People didn't know that the drought was going to last a whole decade. Farmers were "next year" people, meaning that they always hoped that the next year would be better than the last. Right as the drought began, so did what became known as "The Great Plow Up". The Great Plow Up was where farmers tried to plow and plant as much land as they could, so they could get more money. Wheat prices weren't as good as they were a couple of years before. They thought if they could grow more, they'd still make enough money.

No one realized what they were doing to the ground until it was too late. The over plowing ripped up all the native grasses which meant that the soil was loose. Loose soil could be blown or eroded away, taking valuable nutrients with it. Dirt without trees or grass does not hold water very well. All through the 1930's, huge dust storms blew across Kansas and the Midwest.

During the dust storms, it was impossible to go outside without breathing in dirt. Even inside a house, families would wear rags over their faces to try to breathe. Both of my great-grandmothers lived through the dust bowl and passed down their memories from children to grandchildren to great-grandchildren. People that lived through the Dust Bowl had to put wet rags against their windowsills to keep the dust out. When they would go to replace the rags, they would be caked with dust of all colors: red dust from Oklahoma, white dust from the Gypsum Hills in southwestern Kansas, and brown dust from everywhere else. People kept their dishes and cups all turned upside down in the cupboards to try to keep them clean. One of my great-grandmothers remembered her dad crying, because they sometimes had to choose between buying food for their family or food for their cattle.

It took about a decade to find out a way to really stop the Dust Bowl. Many Kansans left for other places. It was too hard to stay. The people who stayed behind to pull our state through were brave, had a lot of hope and courage, and saved our state and its natural beauty. Farmers started strip farming, which is when crops are planted in an alternating pattern. It reminds me of stripes on material, the way it alternates colors. Kansas farmers learned tiered farming, which is like if you made steps in the earth. It helps stop water and soil from running straight off a hill. Kansans dug lakes and ponds, so that when the rain came back, we could hold on to it. Many Kansans planted trees so that when the wind would pick up, the soil would stay secured in its place. Finally, after all of that hard work, the rain came back.

Today, we face similar problems brought on by climate change. Our summers get hotter every year. Winter isn't always cold, but when it is, it can be extremely harsh. Sometimes things heat up or freeze at an unusual time of the year. Finding new ways of farming that use less water, changing the ways we use chemicals, and developing seeds and crops that can live through these extremes are important to our success. Using alternative energy sources, such as wind and solar will help.

Kansans are stubborn; we will figure out a way to solve this new problem. We are friendly, which means we can do it together. Kansans are down-to-earth. We will make sure everyone learns how to use natural resources and agriculture to keep Kansas happy and healthy, and pledge not to turn our backs on Kansas!

Kansas Essay
Jessie Taylor
Grade 8
Iola Middle School

Kansas is a state that some people may look over as one of no importance, but Kansas played a large part in one of the most crucial events in US history: The Civil War. The Civil War is an extremely important event because it resulted in the end of slavery for the United States of America. The state of Kansas is a contributing factor in how the Civil War started. Kansas and its citizens can learn greatly from Kansas's history before the Civil War.

Before Kansas became a state in 1861, a decision had to be made: would it come into the union as a free or slave state? This question was a result of an act passed by Congress on May 30, 1854: the Kansas-Nebraska Act. This act stated that Kansas and Nebraska territories were able to choose whether they wanted to be a pro or anti-slavery state. Immediately following the passage of the Kansas-Nebraska act, supporters for and against slavery looked at Kansas as a valuable state for their slavery stance. Quickly, Kansas became a battleground of guerilla warfare and heated confrontations all about slavery. This time period of turmoil, difficulty, and bloodshed for the future state soon became known as "Bleeding Kansas."

Between the passage of the Kansas-Nebraska Act of 1854 and the start of the Civil War in 1861 is where the events of Bleeding Kansas fit into history. During this time tension was extremely high as both pro and anti-slavery supporters tried as hard as possible to make Kansas a state in support of their stance. Pro-slavery Missourians came into the Kansas territory from the strongly slave state, and northern anti-slavery supporters and abolitionists rushed in as well. Gangs of men from each side quickly began terrorizing each other, pillaging, burning, and destroying property. This violence continued to escalate until the Civil war started in 1861 pushed on by the events of Bleeding Kansas and by other bloody confrontations dealing with slavery.

During the period of Bleeding Kansas, people were divided against each other. Because of their different opinions, they hated each other, and violence and bloodshed were the result. Kansans today can learn much from the events of Bleeding Kansas. Kansans can see how cruelty, violence, and unthoughtfulness can be the result when people with differing opinions are not considerate and respectful of the other side's beliefs and opinions. Kansans can learn to be kind and work together to accomplish what needs to be done. They can learn to simply agree to disagree and be respectful when they find themselves with someone with different opinions than them. Kansans can also learn to look past things of little importance and work together to accomplish more important things that will benefit everyone.

The issue in the period of Bleeding Kansas was slavery. Now that problem is behind us, but Kansans can still learn from the events of Bleeding Kansas. Today there are other topics like school funding, politics, and money that people have very specific opinions on. Although people may feel strongly about their views, and think their opinion is right on these topics, they can still be considerate and respectful of others and their beliefs. Kansans can understand that when disagreements arise, we can handle them with civility and dignity.

The state of Kansas itself can learn from the events of Bleeding Kansas as well. In this period, Kansas was divided against itself and in turmoil. Kansas today can look back and see how easily disagreements can get out of hand and cause violence that hurts everyone: men, women, and children alike. Kansas can learn that it needs to respect everyone, rich or poor, black or white, male or female, and give them their rights and liberty. While it is unlikely that another "Bleeding Kansas" will happen with bloodshed and killing, harsh words and hostility are just as awful and hurtful. Kansas can be a peacemaker state that is firm but kind.

Bleeding Kansas is an event that caused one of the bloodiest wars in U.S. history. Kansas and Kansans alike can learn from these events to be civil and kind. We as Kansans can be respectful to each other and of each others opinions, and Kansas as a state can respect everyone and be a model state to others in our nation. Kansas can look back and learn from Bleeding Kansas, and while the issues were different back then, new and controversial issues are still prevalent in our modern day society that can be put into the same context. Kansas can then learn from the past and not make the same mistakes it did. I believe that Kansas is a great state and that it can be better unified, and stronger if we are respectful and kind. I am proud to be a Kansan and live in the great state of Kansas.

Out of the Ashes: The Referendum for Women's Rights
Elsie Unruh
Grade 8
Hutchinson Middle School

In mythology it is said that the phoenix is immortal, and can live and rise again from the ashes of the fire that had once killed it. In the 1860's a woman's job was to cook and clean, but never to vote or help decide the future of America. In 1867 it seemed impossible for women to do a lot of things, but little did they know of the amazing future to come. Now, because of Kansans trying, sometimes failing, but then trying again, women have the rights that all citizens have today.

In 1867 a woman's life was to cook, clean, marry well, and have lots of children. As a woman, your life was controlled by men. In the 1800's there were few jobs for women other than teaching and that was a low status and low pay job. Most women could not get higher education or good opportunities, because they were not a man.

In 1848 the women's movement first met in New York, and they started to pay attention to the midwestern states. Later in 1861 Kansas started to allow women to vote in local elections. Suffragists such as Mary Jane Ritchie in Topeka, Clarina Nichols and Mary Tenney Gray rallied and fought till eventually in 1867 Kansas became the first state to have a referendum for voting rights. This referendum was for not just for women; it proposed all citizens could vote, male, female, black, white.

After all the hard work, unfortunately the referendum was denied by white male voters. The Kansas women's movement was shaken, it felt like this was just another way for men to control their life. But just like the phoenix, the spirit of freedom and equal rights was still alive in their hearts. They refused to give up. But this would not be the last time the phoenix would go to the fire. In 1894 they took the referendum back to the people to fight for another day. Once again the male voters shut them down.

Instead of giving up these women went back to work, their fiery gaze switched to local elections. The Kansas Equal Suffrage Association realized that women may not be able to vote in national elections, but they worked to allow women to vote in local elections and to run for office as town officials. "National leaders saw the newly organized western territories and states as ideal battlegrounds for women's rights in America. Kansas women saw some early victories; they gained the right to vote in school district elections in 1861 and municipal elections in 1887."

Susanna Salter moved to Kansas in 1872. In April 1887 she was put on the ballot in Argonia for mayor of the town by men as a joke. She won the election with two-thirds of the vote. "She did not realize her name was on the ballot until the morning of the election!" This was a huge breakthrough for the women's rights movement. She was Mayor for one term (one year), and did not run again. The point was made, and through that year there were no problems. She was the first female mayor in the United States.

The first phoenix was born in 1867, it was thrown back into the fire, then a second was born in 1894. But the phoenix was once again burned by the flames of prejudice. Finally for the third time the phoenix was set to soar. On November fifth of 1912 the referendum was a success. The Sunflower State was shining almost as bright as the fire that lit her eyes. According to Kansapedia, "With the tide of reform running high during the first two decades of the 20th century, the campaign for women's suffrage took on new life." Kansas became the 8th state to allow full suffrage to women. After this success they didn't give up. They kept working hard and fighting for rights for all women.

Finally after Kansas women got the right to vote, the rest of America did. On August 8, 1920, the long sought after goal was achieved. The United States ratified the 19th Amendment to the United States Constitution.

Because of the work that the women's suffrage movement did in Kansas, America would not be the same. The first impact was that it showed other states that Kansas would fight for equal opportunities. Even though the first referendum lost, it inspired other states. After the referendum the National American Woman Suffrage Association decided to make the Sunflower their emblem of the suffrage campaign.

Because Kansas held their referendum so early in the battle for suffrage it shows that Kansans are forward thinkers, have new ideas, and want equal opportunities for all. That was shown also in the abolitionist movement. As time goes on there will be more issues that Kansans will fight for, but may be shut down again and again; the 1867 referendum shows that even if you are burned like the phoenix, you can rise from the ashes and try again until you finally win.

Cyclops, Kleagles, Wizards and Willopses-wallopuses
Jacob Unruh
Grade 10
Hutchinson High School

William Allen White was born in 1868 in Emporia, Kansas. He moved to El Dorado as a young boy, and as a teenager worked as a press apprentice, where he developed his passion for journalism. He went to Emporia University and Kansas University, before marrying Sallie Moss Lindsay, who was a teacher. Together, they bought the Emporia Gazette. White garnered attention when he wrote an editorial entitled "What's the Matter with Kansas?" in 1896, criticizing the populist movement in Kansas for hurting the state's economy. White continued as an editor at the Gazette, occasionally writing on political matters. He earned a Pulitzer Prize in 1923 for writing "To an Anxious Friend," which argued for free speech. In the early 1920's, the Ku Klux Klan attracted White's attention and vitriol.

The KKK first entered Kansas in 1921, and an article from the Emporia Gazette in 2014 states that by 1924, around ten thousand Emporians were members of the Klan. The mayor of Emporia at that time was a supporter of the KKK. The police force was also dominated by Klansmen, who used their power to forcefully remove journalists from meetings. White noticed the rise of the Klan, and with great concern told newspaperman Charles Scott in 1923, "No arguments you may use, no facts you may present, no logic you may array will in the slightest affect these people. They have no capacity for receiving argument, no minds for retaining or sifting facts and no mental processes that will hold logic. If they had any of these things they wouldn't be Kluxers."

Kansas was due for a Governor's election in 1924. Ben Paulen, a conservative, won the Republican primary, because the anti-Klan vote was split among multiple candidates. Paulen was accused of having ties to the Klan. As a chairman in the Republican party, Paulen blocked resolutions denouncing the Klan, who fully embraced Paulen. Photos of the candidate could be found at Klan offices. On the Democratic side, candidate Jonathan Davis was impartial to the Klan, treating the movement as a non-issue.

William Allen White wanted an anti-KKK candidate to win the governorship, so he tried to convince Senator Joseph Bristow and former Governor Walter Stubbs to run, but failed to do so. As a last-ditch effort to bring attention to the issue, White started considering a run of his own. The book William Allen White's America states that while he was initially on the fence, what finally pushed White to make an announcement was a letter he received from a Jewish merchant. The note said that because of the Klan, the merchant's business was struggling, his wife was ostracized socially, and his children were being mistreated. White sent out a petition to get a sense of support for a potential campaign. He needed two and a half thousand signatures to be officially recognized as an independent. He ended up getting over ten thousand, which was even more impressive considering that none of the signatures were from his home provinces of Lyons and Emporia.

On September 22nd, 1924, White announced his gubernatorial run in front of a crowd of around 1,500 people in Cottonwood Falls. A newspaper article from the Topeka Daily Capital reports that he gave a stirring speech where he made clear that the central theme of his campaign was going to be the condemnation of the Klan. His campaign slogan was tolerance. White denounced the Klan for their hold on Kansas politics.

He claimed that the KKK used their influence to nominate Paulen as the Republican candidate, saying, "The Klan knows no politics, it knows no religion and it knows no morals. But it ganged and gagged the Kansas primaries." He went on to eloquently state that "The Cyclops, Kleagles, Wizards and Willopses-wallopuses began parading in the Kansas cow pastures, passing the word down to the shirt-tail rangers they were to go into the Kansas primaries and nominate Ben Paulen."

The main argument from the KKK at this point in time was that they prioritized Americanism over everything, and that blacks, Jews, and Catholics could not be truly American. White's response was that "When a man lays down his life for his country he is 100 per cent (sic) American though he is Jew or Negro. Why, then, should he have to die to prove his Americanism?" White believed that the way to combat the KKK's hateful tactics were by acting with reason, not force. To spit fire, not light fire. The Klan clearly felt otherwise, because after the speech, they burned a cross and sent threats to White and his supporters.

As the race went on, White established other policies he supported, such as promising to appoint women to state agency positions, amending child labor laws, and providing aid to hospitals with maternity wards. He toured the state, with his son as chauffeur since he was a notoriously bad driver. The KKK, however, was still White's main focus. As he stated in his announcement letter in the Emporia Gazette, "I want to be governor to free Kansas from the disgrace of the Ku Klux Klan. ... The thought that Kansas should have a government beholden to this hooded gang of masked fanatics, ignorant and tyrannical in their ruthless oppression, is what calls me out of the pleasant ways of my life into this distasteful but necessary task."

While many, including White, believed that his chances of actually winning the Governorship was slim, he was still lauded and criticized for bringing attention to the Klan, both in Kansas and nationally as his support grew. When all was said and done, White received 149,811 votes, losing to both Paulen, who got 323,403, and Davis, who garnered 182,861. However, candidates that White supported, such as Attorney. General Charles B. Griffith, Secretary of State Frank J. Ryan, and State Superintendent of Public Instruction Jess W. Miley, defeated opposition from pro-Klan candidates. These state positions became critical when Attorney General Griffith opposed granting a charter to the Klan in Kansas, effectively banning the organization from the state. White's impact on Kansas also appeared on a personal level. On November 11, 1924, White wrote that he had received a letter from a Jew who had told him that because of his campaign bringing attention to the Klan, it was a whole different atmosphere for himself and his children. White said that "The fact that I could get out and spit in the face of the Klan ... had cleared up the atmosphere, and had sent people in his home town to his defense... I am very proud of it all."

White continued to be active in his condemnation of the Klan up until his death, which ironically enough was on Kansas day in 1944. The Emporia Gazette is still run by the White family to this day, and the White legacy lives on through the annual children's book award presented in his name.

Despite the fact that White ran a losing campaign, he had great success in reducing the influence of the Ku Klux Klan both in Kansas and in the United States. White proved that we can fight bigotry with reason instead of with weapons. Through his journalistic experience, his skills as a rhetorician, and his nobility to do his civic duty in the face of hardship, White was able to make a positive impact in people's lives and our democracy.

As Kansans, we need to remember that when there is a threat to our common good, we should stay involved in public service and activism. It takes courage and perseverance, but through hard work comes great social change. Politics should not be a cynical game where millionaires fight to better their own selfish interests, but rather a system in which passionate civilians can create change in their communities.

The Greenburg Tornado
Kai Waddell
Grade 4
Clark Davidson Elementary School

About the Greensburg Tornado

On May 4, 2007 during a deadly outbreak of tornados, the city of Greensburg Kansas fell in the path of an EF5 tornado which destroyed 95% of the city and left 5% severely damaged. The Big Well was home to a 1,000 pallasite meteorite which was moved around and found in the rubble after the tornado hit. Around 1,500 people had to evacuate but still it killed 11 people between the ages of 46 to 84. After the tornado, Greensburg became a green town, leading some to call it the 'Greenest in America'. LEED (Leadership Energy and Environmental Design) gave them LEED platinum status based on their new designs which they earned for having 80 points or higher on their strict grading scale. They were the first city in the nation to earn LEED platinum and become the greenest town.

What we can learn

We should research tornados and invent devices to improve warnings and possibly save lives. There should be sirens at more locations to get the word out to people that there is danger. This would allow the warning to travel a farther distance in a shorter time. Easier access to shelters should be made so that people take less time and are able to get to safety faster when an emergency hits. We can always repair the damage that a tornado has caused. The new buildings can be made with stronger materials that are environmentally friendly and can survive a tornado. Cities like the new Greensburg are good for the environment. They have wind powered turbines and solar power to make the environment a better place by not using coal, oil or harmful gasses. Greensburg becoming an environmentally friendly town could encourage other cities to build green. They could set an example to other cities to let them see what the other effects of a green town are and helping them learn from their mistakes. In May 2012, the citizens rebuilt the Big Well museum and put pieces of rubble inside to honor the old city of Greensburg so that the past would not be forgotten.

What Kansas can take going forward

After the damage caused to Greensburg, we know what an EF5 is capable of. We can make stronger shelters and update our safety preparations. Food, water and first aid kits should be in the shelters in case they are needed. When buildings are demolished or destroyed, we can build more LEED and environmentally friendly buildings. We can find more sustainable resources like wind, sun and electric power. These resources can be used to power cars, appliances, buildings, lights and all sorts of other things without using any resources that can destroy the planet. If every state created just one green city that would tremendously help the planet by not using bad resources and educated people how to live better.

Tornadoes
Samson Weber
Grade 5
Silver Lake Grade School

Swirling funnels, dirt and trees flying everywhere, cars, animals, and houses being tossed recklessly by the strong wind are all images that people think about when they hear the word tornado. Growing up in Kansas, a state in tornado alley, I've heard about tornadoes all my life. My mom and dad always like to tell my sister and I the story about a time when I was four and my sister was still a baby. We were all out having a picnic at Lake Shawnee in Topeka, KS when all of a sudden the weather changed. It was a wonderful, sunny afternoon, but the sky darkened and one of my aunts spotted a funnel cloud headed in our direction. My parents tell us about how they had to grab us and get to safety as quickly as we could. Normally, you think of heading to the basement, but during that storm our parents took us to a huge drainage ditch to hide from the storm. That tornado like most that I've heard about didn't do too much damage. While this is a big story for my parents and seemed like a scary storm to me, this is nothing compared to the F5 tornado that Hesston, KS experienced in 1990. Those living in Hesston, KS that day never dreamt about what they would experience, but this tornado wrecked their town and changed their perspectives of tornadoes forever.

Kansas was not prepared for what kind of tornado was coming on March 13th, 1990. This was the third day for severe weather in the Midwest area. Tornadoes had been popping up from a storm front that stretched from Texas to Nebraska. At about 4:30 p.m. a large tornado was reported moving northeast about a mile south of Castleton, KS. This tornado stretched over a half mile wide and lasted for over two hours. This tornado was one that seemed to keep regenerating. It would seem to narrow down and then widen back out. The tornado entered Harvey County 8 miles southwest of Burrton, and this is where it killed a six year old boy. Dixie Fisher, her three sons Lucas, Brandon, and Garrett and their grandparents all went to the basement for safety. After the tornado passed, it was discovered that a tree had hit the chimney of the house, the chimney fell and crushed the little six year old Lucas to death. At about 5:30 p.m. the tornado siren started in Hesston, KS. 60 people were injured. The local Pizza Hut manager took as many customers as he could into the walk in refrigerator for protection. There was 25 million dollars in damage in Harvey county alone. 60 people were injured, and 226 homes and 21 businesses were damaged or destroyed. After devastating Hesston, the tornado continued moving northeast where it actually ended up merging with another tornado. After the storm, a check from a Hesston business was found about 85 miles away in Manhattan, KS where it had been dropped by the storm.

This storm was horrific and caused horrible damage, but Kansans were fast to act during and after the disaster. The community as well as outside volunteers got to work the very next day on cleaning and rebuilding. In fact, the Pizza Hut was rebuilt in only three weeks. This tornado was also different from others because this was one of the first tornados to be photographed and recorded by so many people. At this time, many people had their own video recorders so it is a highly documented tornado. Hesston will always remember this day not only because of the damage left behind, but also because of the growth the town experienced after. The city has steadily grown since the tornado and now the city is trying to make sure that they preserve the stories of the tornado survivors.

Even though it has almost been thirty years since this tragic tornado devastated this small Kansas town, this is a moment in Kansas history that will be remembered forever. If you haven't heard of this tornado, you can go to Youtube and easily find a video to see how gigantic and terrifying this storm truly was. Now when the tornado siren blares, Hesston and all Kansas residents have a greater appreciation and sense of urgency to get to safety than they did before

Barbed Wire: The End of the West
Brendan C. Wheatley
Grade 7
Frontier Trail Middle School

Kansas is full of modern inventions and great companies, like Garmin in Olathe, and aircraft manufacturers in Wichita. Even in its early days, Kansas lead the way in the westward expansion. With all the people heading west, they needed to find ways to cope with the flat, baron landscape. People would have to search across the land if they wanted to build things like fences, houses, wagons, et cetera. They had to think outside the box in order to do this effectively. Luckily, there were a lot of great thinkers in Kansas.

It is the year 1870 and cattle roam freely across the Kansas plains. They are brought in cattle drives to booming cow towns like Abilene and Dodge City, or lead by cowboys to the feeding grounds in the Flint Hills or Kansa Prairie. Everything was working out well, but when farmers tried to keep their cows in their own fenced in pastures, the cattle would often escape and trample nearby crops, or the cattle could be stolen by jealous neighbors. Some people tried to use wires to keep cows in a confined pasture, but it was ineffective against the weight and stubbornness of the cattle. A clever entrepreneur decided to do something about this.

In 1873, Joseph Glidden twisted two wires together, and wrapped a barb between them. He patented his design after its successful showing at the Illinois State Fair (paragraph 2 of "Joseph Glidden Applies For Patent On His Barbed Wire Design" History.com). Millions of people wanted to purchase his revolutionary barbed wire. He and one other barbed wire innovator created the Barb Fence Company of DeKalb, Illinois.

Following the creation of the wire, ranchers of the west started fencing up their land with the cheap "devils rope" and began keeping more cattle. Open ranges became pastures and there were more ranchers than ever flocking west. Farmers seldom worried about cows trampling their crops, and ranchers didn't need to hire cowboys to keep their cows safe.

This affected the entire world in some way, but in Kansas it was different. A majority of Kansans' lifestyles were changed forever. In its early days, the state of Kansas had many cow towns (the most famous being Dodge City), that relied on the movement of cattle as their income. Lots of people made their living being cowboys or cowhands, selling products to cowboys, and transporting cattle. After barbed wire came along, these kinds of jobs were no longer necessary, and most of those who worked in the cattle industry were out of business. Prices of pasture land also increased by over 50%, because much less land was needed to keep cattle in check.(paragraph 8 of "Barbed Wire Entrepreneurship" by Daniel Benjamin, Perc.org)

As a result of all the confined pasture land, the Plains were being overgrazed by the cattle, and the prairie environment was changing into a more dry, lifeless grassland (excluding all the cows). Because of all the flat, dry land, wind blew without stopping, and picked up dust and dirt. That became one of the countless factors that caused the dust bowl of the early 1930's that ravaged western Kansas (paragraph 4 of "Barbed Wire Entrepreneurship" Daniel Benjamin, Perc.org)

Although there were many negative effects of the barbed wire, there were also a lot of positives. Barbed wire completely changed the cattle industry from expensively transporting the cattle across the plains, to keeping them in cheap pastures with little to no need of supervision. More cows could be kept, and more beef produced. Cattle also became cheaper, since they were now widely available. The cows were now swarming over the plains like the buffalo that once dominated the landscape.

This is proof of the lasting effect of barbed wire on Kansas, America, and the world. Unfortunately, barbed wire nowadays is greatly overlooked as a boring and simple piece of farm equipment that has no value or use, but it's amazing contributions and elaborate history say otherwise. This simple creation caused so much change in Kansas, and it started as a way to keep cows from breaking through the fence, and ended up modernizing the west. If everybody thought of a solution to even the smallest problems, than the greatest problems could be solved, and the entire world could be changed.

The idea of putting a touch screen on a cell phone ended up connecting the whole Earth with each other, and allowing us access to almost all information. The concept of a "buggy" that is driven with no horses allowed us to travel further distances than ever, faster than ever. All of these innovations that change the world started as a simple idea in the back of someone's mind, that became reality using a little bit of creativity. Kansas may not seem like it, but it's full of very creative minds. If all of Kansas' creative people decided to work together, than Kansas could become the center of global progress toward the future. It is the year 1873, the year barbed wire arose. The year that brought about the end of the west, but the beginning of Kansas' advancement.

Citations

https://www.thoughtco.com/history-of-barbed-wire-1991330 by Mary Bellis, March 1, 2019 https://www.history.com/this-day-in-history/joseph-glidden-applies-for-a-patent-on-his-barbed-wire-design by History.com Editors, December 13, 2018

https://m.youtube.com/watch?v=Cw6BVLcOqhk. November 21, 2011

https://www.perc.org/2011/02/24/barbed-wire-entrepreneurship/. Daniel Benjamin, February 24, 2011

https://historyengine.richmond.edu/episodes/view/6265. University of Richmond 2015

https://militaryhistorynow.com/2014/01/08/barbed-wire-war-how-one-farmers-innovation-changed-the-battlefield/ January 8 2014. MilitaryHistoryNow.com

https://www.britannica.com/biography/Joseph-Farwell-Glidden Encyclopedia britannica editors.

Shawnee Methodist Mission
Ben Wieland
Grade 10
Mill Valley High School

Sparsely scattered across my hometown of Shawnee Mission, Kansas are innocuous wooden signs. Tucked away beside crowded roads or hidden alongside park trails, they're nigh-impossible to notice — and even harder to care about. However, once in a blue moon, I stop to read one.

In white print lettering bordered by painted sunflowers, the signs denote "Kansas Historical Markers." They tell tales of brave settlers conquering the Wild West, crossing the prairie searching for a new life.

There is one marker about my hometown of Shawnee Mission's namesake: the Shawnee Methodist Mission. The Shawnee Methodist Mission, according to the state's sign, "was attended mainly by Indian orphans" who received "elementary schooling, religious instruction, and training in agriculture and domestic arts."

That is the Shawnee Methodist Mission the state wanted Kansans to believe in when these historical markers were commissioned in the mid-1900s. That is not the real Shawnee Methodist Mission.

Here is the story of the real Shawnee Methodist Mission.

To understand the Shawnee Methodist Mission, we must first understand its victims: the Shawnee. For what historians estimate to be millenia, the tribe's members lived in harmony with one another and neighboring tribes; the European colonizers had not yet stolen their way of life. Then came so-called "explorers," carrying Old World bacteria; a Pandora's box of death and disease was unleashed upon the tribe. The once-plentiful membership of the Shawnee plummeted. The violent process of colonization had begun.

Still, the Shawnee pressed on. Their population, shrunken by smallpox to a tenth of its former size, still, at least, had the land and the buffalo to survive by.

Centuries passed. Conflicts came and went. Countries were formed. The Shawnee survived.

Then, a demagogue named Andrew Jackson over a thousand miles away took matters into his own hands. It was time for a new form of colonization: Manifest Destiny. To clear land for the so-called American Dream to spread, Jackson's government decided the tribes - the Shawnee - would have to go.

Jackson ignored his own Supreme Court to offer tribes an ultimatum. Adapt to American culture or get out of the way. The Shawnee refused to get out of the way.

The stage was set for the Shawnee Methodist Mission to victimize the Shawnee, to kill the tribe's culture in the name of God.

The Kansas state sign tells travelers that young Indian orphans at the Shawnee Methodist Mission were given "elementary schooling, religious instruction, and training in agriculture and domestic arts." The mission's founder Thomas Johnson would certainly give a very different definition of his goal.

Johnson, like the other missionaries of his time, had one goal and one goal only: to follow what he believed to be the word of God and convert as many people as possible to Christianity. The wishes of those non-believers, in this case the Shawnee tribe, were ignored. When the Shawnee refused to peacefully give up their culture and history, Johnson turned to less godly measures.

Other missionaries who grew frustrated with their failure to quickly convert new Christians forced tribe members to build churches. This slavery, sanitized with terms like "establishing the mission," was described by one historian as equivalent to "forced movement of black people from Africa to the American South" in terms of the cruelty inflicted.

This de facto slavery wasn't the only harm inflicted on tribes like the Shawnee by missionaries. Once members of a tribe entered a mission area, they weren't allowed to leave. They forced discrimination from religious members of the mission and were beaten for refusing to follow Christian culture. One historian at the time wrote that mission leaders considered the native tribes "too much a child, too much a slave, too little a man."

Now, Thomas Johnson's Shawnee Methodist Mission could've been the exception rather than the rule. He may have treated the Shawnee well, and treated them as equals. However, all existing evidence points to the contrary. Johnson was a proud slave owner, so he clearly had no qualms with forcing others to obey him, and the fact that no Shawnee still practice their native culture in Shawnee Mission, Kansas proves that this mission was no better than the rest.

The Kansas government, to their credit, did an excellent job of hiding this secret abuse and destruction of tribal culture. History is written by the winners, and all the state-produced literature available online about the Shawnee Methodist Mission and Thomas Johnson paints a heroic picture. Shawnee Mission is located today in Johnson County. This whitewashing of Kansas history is nearly impossible to escape.

In a twist of irony, another "Kansas Historical Marker" lists threats that the American colonizers faced while moving westward; in other words, threats faced while stealing the land, livelihood, and culture of the Shawnee tribe. One of the threats listed is "the constant threat of Indian attack."

It is hard to live with this. Me and the other 65,000 Kansans living in Shawnee Mission have endorsed the theft of Shawnee tribal land and the destruction of Shawnee tribal culture. We're "Johnson County folks," known by the last name of a slave owner who eradicated the Shawnee in the name of God. However, we Kansans can use our terrible history to grow and become better in the future.

We can learn that the attitudes that justified westward expansion are immoral and evil. Seeing ourselves as superior to others because we are Americans has failed time and time again. Putting our state ahead of other states or other countries has failed. Any misguided American exceptionalism here in Kansas leads to us betraying our moral values.

If we ignore the lessons of the Shawnee Methodist Mission atrocities, we become modern-day Thomas Johnsons, acting not in the name of God but in the name of America or the name of Kansas. We justify atrocities and human rights violations, this time not against the outsider Shawnee tribe but against outsiders all around the world. We exclude those who don't adapt to our antiquated idea of "American" — those of different races, religions, and places of birth. We become just the next generation of colonialist thinkers, believing that we should force our way of life onto everybody else. We become racists, sexists, and bigots. We become the embodiment of hate.

It doesn't have to be that way.

As Kansans, we uniquely have an opportunity to atone for past atrocities. Where Thomas Johnson saw outsiders as inferior, we can see them as equals. Where Thomas Johnson stood his ground and refused to change his way of life, we can grow into better moral human beings.

It's also not enough to talk the talk of equality and

tolerance. We Kansans must walk the walk as well. Belief means nothing without action. We must vote for candidates who protect the rights of everybody, not just Kansans or Americans. We must advocate for policies to allow those who are not like us to keep their ways of life. We must act to destroy our deserved reputation as colonizers, as excluders, as bullies of the world.

Our past is ugly. The atrocities of the Shawnee Methodist Mission are ugly. However, we must not hide these atrocities of the past. Bring the evil, the darkness, into the light. Then act to ensure the darkness cannot return to our state forever. Defeating our darkness will make Kansas's future even brighter.

Kansas Essay
Maggie Wieland
Grade 6
Monticello Trails Middle School

When most people think of *Brown vs Board of Education*, they picture the US Supreme Court. What some people don't know is that it all started right here in Topeka, Kansas. Oliver Brown was an African American man living in Topeka. His daughter, Linda Brown, went to school at Monroe Elementary. Monroe Elementary was just fine, but it was a mile away and Sumner Elementary was an all- white school just four blocks away from their home. When Oliver Brown tried to enroll his daughter at Sumner Elementary, he was told to enroll at Monroe instead. At this time the policy for public schools was "separate, but equal" which meant the schools could be segregated if they were getting the same quality schools and education.

He decided to sue the Topeka Board of Education for violation of the 14th amendment. The 14th amendment states that any US citizen gets equal protection under the law. The reason he sued was not that he thought Monroe was inferior to Sumner. The circumstances were what angered the parents of Linda Brown the most.

On the day of the trial Robert Carter, his lawyer argued in the name of Oliver Brown. Robert Carter stated, "…because the act of separation and the act of segregation in and of itself denies them equal educational opportunities which the Fourteenth Amendment secures." Carter also stated later in his testimony that it, "lowered their level of aspiration."

The Supreme Court of The United States ruled unanimously that as said by Earl Warren, "in the field of public schools the doctrine 'separate, but equal' has no place."

When Brown was asked why he wanted to join the lawsuit he said, "The entire colored race is craving the light, and the only way to reach the light is to start our children together in their infancy and they come up together."

I think that Kansans today can learn from this because today some parents think that they are keeping their kids safe by keeping their kids at schools that only really have their child's race. We should be exposing our children to different races from a young age.

Although segregation is no longer legal there is very clear segregation at our public schools. If you look at the numbers, it says that the Kansas City Public School District racial make-up is 57% black or African American, 28% Hispanic, 9% white, and 6% other. It also says that one in every five kids' primary language is not English. I am part of the USD 232 school district and our districts racial make-up is 92% white, 1.9% Black or African American, 2.1% Asian, and 4.7% Hispanic. This shows that while our schools are not legally segregated, it is almost as if they are because of how out of place and African American student might feel if they came to our school. I think Kansas could work on making our communities more welcoming to people of other races so our students can be growing up in a more diverse environment. I know I would love it if we had more African American or Hispanic students at our school!

Obviously, you are not going to only ever work with people who have the same race as you so it should not feel awkward or different. If kids are used to working with people of other races it will help them succeed more in their future.

In conclusion, having more diverse schools will only lead to more learning and more success. It will not only be good for students, but also for our communities because it will give them the opportunity to learn about cultures that they otherwise would never learn about. This would only have a positive impact on both our schools and communities.

Turkey Red Seed
Zachary Wieland
Grade 3
Prairie Ridge Elementary School

Have you ever heard of the Turkey Red seed? It may sound like it but it does not grow turkey. It actually grows winter wheat. So do you know how we got it? We got from immigrants; to be specific, we got it from Mennonites who came to Kansas from Russia.

In 1874 there were people called Mennonites who came to practice their religion freely. In exchange for the right to practice religion freely, they gave us the Turkey Red seed. The reason the Turkey Red seed was important was that farmers in Kansas could harvest the wheat before the locusts came and devoured it. The immigration of the Russian Mennonites in 1874 was an important event in Kansas history because if we hadn't got that seed, Kansans in 1874 wouldn't have had enough food to survive.

Kansans of today can learn an important lesson from the immigration of the Russian Mennonites in 1874. Today, people are afraid of immigrants but why?
Could their culture change our culture? It could but maybe we need change. Could they "steal our jobs"? Is it really stealing or do they provide better services than we do? Do we really need a wall for keeping immigrants out of our country? But then we ask -- is it our country? Why does Donald Trump call immigrants animals? Is he afraid of them or is he towering over them?

As for me, one of my best friend's parents are immigrants from Africa and he and his family have brought a lot of good things in my life.

So a way that that could help Kansas take a step forward is if we supported immigrants because if they help us, why couldn't we help them. We have to think about the good things immigrants bring not just the bad.

That is why we should remember the Russian Mennonite immigrants and the Turkey Red seed as Kansas moves forward into the future.

Reviewers for Kansas Book Festival Writing Contest 2019

Peggy Crubel
Kim Young
Katie Ewert
Ethel Edwards
Beth Dobler
Carmaine Ternes
Andrea Marshbank
Steve Ternes
Sarah Perryman
Terri Wojtakewicz
Roy Bird
Shana Schmidt
Brady Johnson

History of the Kansas Book Festival

The Kansas Book Festival, under its current leadership, began in 2011 with First Lady Mary Brownback. The first event was held Saturday, September 24, at the Kansas Historical Society in Topeka. Approximately 900 were in attendance to hear more than thirty authors, including David Eisenhower, present their most recent books. Since then, attendance has grown to more than 2,000 people. Authors such as WWII Navajo Code Talker Chester Nez, Joel Rosenberg, Alexandra Robbins, Clare Vanderpool, Frank White and Sara Paretsky have joined us for author presentations and signings.

In March 2012, the first round of Kansas Book Festival Library Grants were awarded with a total of nearly $15,000 being distributed to public and school libraries across the State. We've now been able to distribute more than $60,000 with the next round of monies being awarded in March 2016. This was also the first year for the KBF Writing Contest which ran from January 1 through April 30.

The Kansas Book Festival Board of Directors was formed at the beginning of 2013 to help ensure the longevity of the Kansas Book Festival Foundation. They meet quarterly to discuss ways to improve the Foundation as a whole, and the Festival.

Mary Brownback

KANSAS MASONIC LITERACY CENTER

Campus Box 4036 • 1 Kellogg Circle • Emporia, KS 66801-5415 • Phone: 620.341.5240 • www.emporia.edu/literacy

Authors,

Henry David Thoreau said, "Not that the story need be long, but it will take a long while to make it short."

Writing is one of the learned skills that comprise literacy. It is a primary way of communicating our thoughts, questions, hopes and dreams. That communication may be to ourselves through writing in a journal, or to others in a letter, email, text message or some form of social media. However, it is conveyed it should be clear and to the point. Of course, it should be proofread with appropriate corrections made before one mails or hits the send button.

Congratulations to our winning authors of the 2019 Kansas Book Festival Young Writers Essay Contest. Keep writing because it is the only way to keep improving your power of communication.

Sincerely,

Dennis J. Kear

Dennis J. Kear, Executive Director
Kansas Masonic Literacy Center

EMPORIA STATE
UNIVERSITY

Ellen Plumb's City Bookstore

1122 Commercial
Emporia, KS 66801
(620) 208-BOOK (2665)
www.ellenplumbs.com

Ellen Plumb opened Emporia's first bookstore in 1870. Her family helped found the city of Emporia. One of the first two graduates of the Kansas State Normal School (now Emporia State University), Miss Plumb was always ahead of her time--and the original spirit of "Locally owned. Fiercely independent." in our town. Nearly a century and a half later, it's our goal to honor her legacy and love of literature.

Kellogg Press

Kevin Rabas
Kansas Poet Laureate 2017-2019

Ronda Miller
President, Kansas Authors Club

Kellogg Press's Mission is to give an uncensored voice to Kansas Authors like Kevin Rabas and Ronda Miller. To purchase books or learn more about us, visit kelloggpress.com.

To order additional copies of the 2019 Kansas Book Festival Yearbook, please visit the secure store at

kellogpress.com

www.ingramcontent.com/pod-product-compliance
Lightning Source LLC
Chambersburg PA
CBHW050438010526
44118CB00013B/1587